COMPOSER SHOWCASE
HAL LEONARD
STUDENT PIANO LIBRARY

Jazz Fest

ORIGINAL PIANO SOLOS IN VARIOUS JAZZ STYLES

BY BILL BOYD

T0040917

CONTENTS

ISBN 978-0-7935-1996-5

HAL•LEONARD®
CORPORATION
7777 W. BLUEMOUND RD. P.O. BOX 13819 MILWAUKEE, WI 53213

Copyright © 1988 by HAL LEONARD CORPORATION
International Copyright Secured   All Rights Reserved

Visit Hal Leonard Online at
www.halleonard.com

FOREWORD

The compositions in this book were written to acquaint the student with various jazz idioms and pianistic devices characteristic of each style. Many styles are represented in this collection of intermediate piano solos, and I hope that students will enjoy exploring the milti-faceted world of jazz piano by studying and performing them.

- THE LOVE ROCK presents rhythm patterns found in the pop-rock ballads of today.

- PERFECT ACHORD is a study in chord voicing.

- SWING STREET uses pentatonic scales which were frequently used by pianists in the swing era.

- THE JAZZ LINE provides an example of an improvised jazz solo and EVERYBODY'S BLUES demonstrates a basic blues-chord progression and chord voicings.

- The fast and slow jazz-waltz are represented by THREE, FOUR – SHUT THE DOOR and A LITTLE JAZZ WALTZ.

- A MINOR CONTRIBUTION is an example of swing-style jazz in a minor key.

- ANDY'S BLUES is a six-eight blues feeling with many right-hand melodic voicings characteristic of this style.

- Finally, VERY BASS(IE) illustrates a left-hand bass line often employed in jazz compositions.

BILL BOYD

INTRODUCTION

The compositions in this book are written in several jazz styles . . . . rock, swing, blues and jazz waltz. Each style requires a certain type of eighth note interpretation. Generally, slow ballads, rock and pieces in six eight time are played with even eighth notes as in classical music. Uneven eighth notes are played in swing and modern jazz compositions. A more precise explanation of eighth note performance appears in the box below.

PERFORMANCE NOTES

SWING EIGHTH NOTES

Eighth notes in swing style jazz are written evenly as in classical music but are played **unevenly.** Practice the following exercises to learn the proper performance of swing eighth notes.

Play and count eighth note triplets.

Count: 1 trip - let 2 trip - let 3 trip - let 4

Tie the first two notes of the triplet together. The resulting rhythm is the swing eighth note feeling.

Count: 1 trip - let 2 trip - let 3 trip - let 4

The triplet rhythm with the first two notes tied together may also be notated in the following manner.

Count: 1 trip - let 2 trip - let 3 trip - let 4

Once the swing eight note "feeling" is achieved, the counting may revert back to "one and two and etc."

Count: 1 and 2 and 3 and 4

On your music, you'll see the following indication:

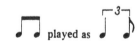

ROCK EIGHTH NOTES

In the rock or slow ballad styles, the notes are played evenly as in classical music.

On your music, you'll see the following indication:

EVERYBODY'S BLUES

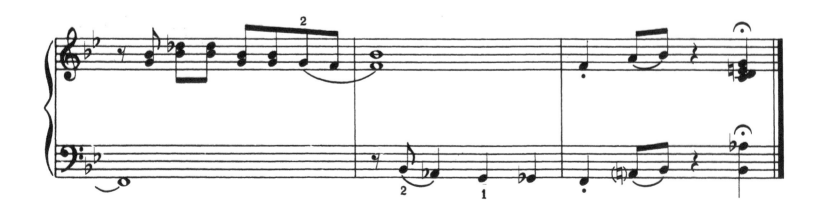

THREE, FOUR — SHUT THE DOOR!

ANDY'S BLUES

Slow Blues (feel in 2)

A MINOR CONTRIBUTION

A LITTLE JAZZ WALTZ

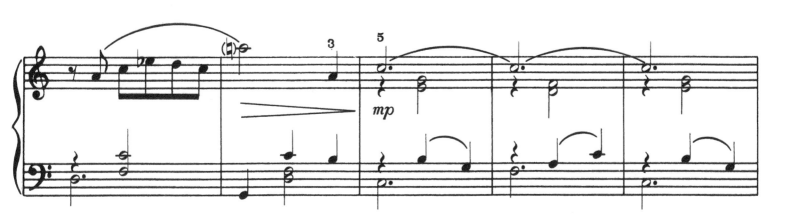

THE LOVE ROCK

VERY BASS(IE)

PERFECT ACHORD

Moderate Bossa Nova (play ♪♪ evenly)

with pedal

THE JAZZ LINE

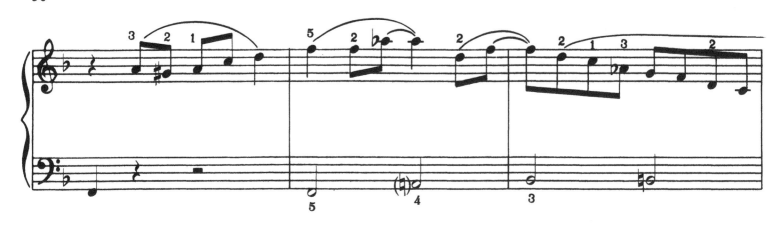

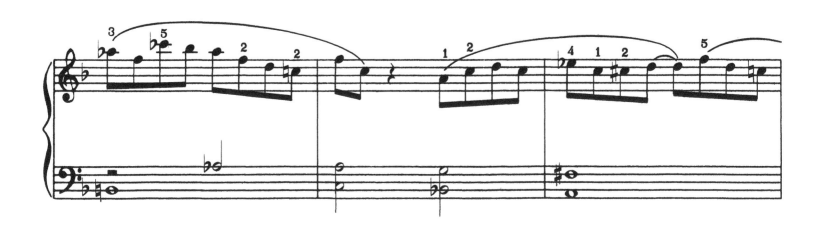

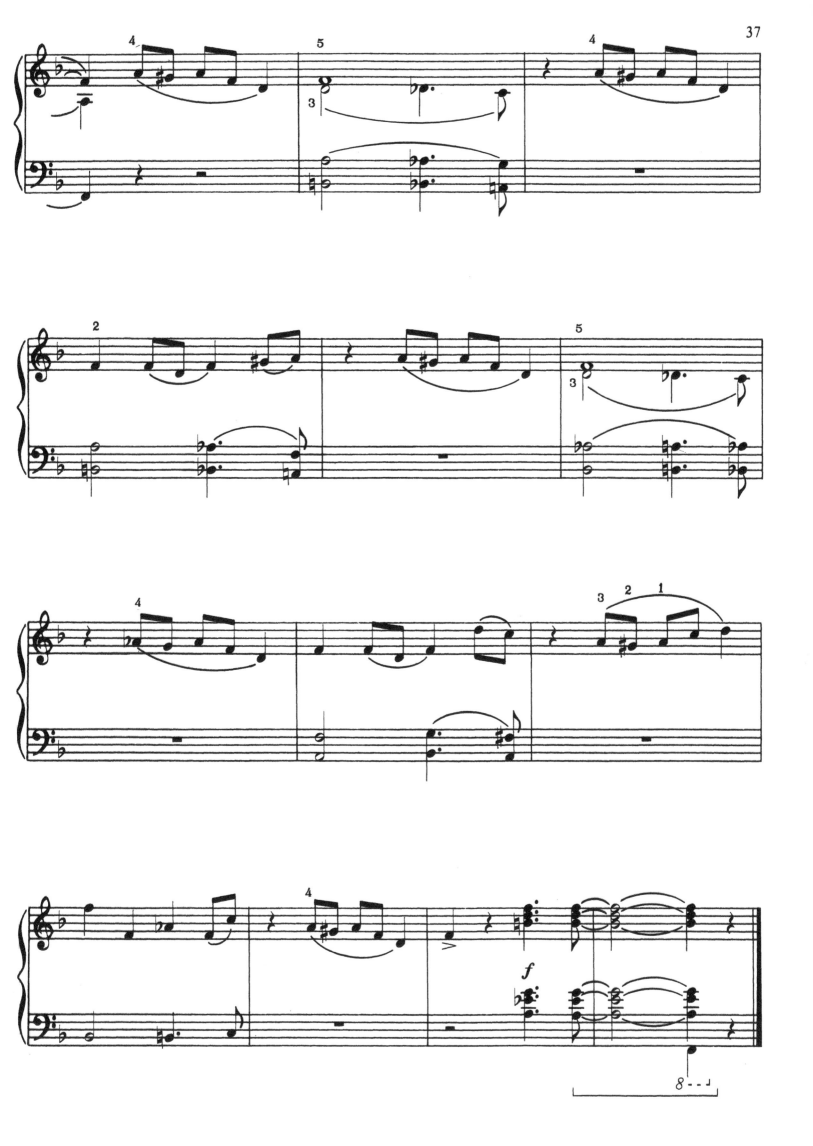

SWING STREET

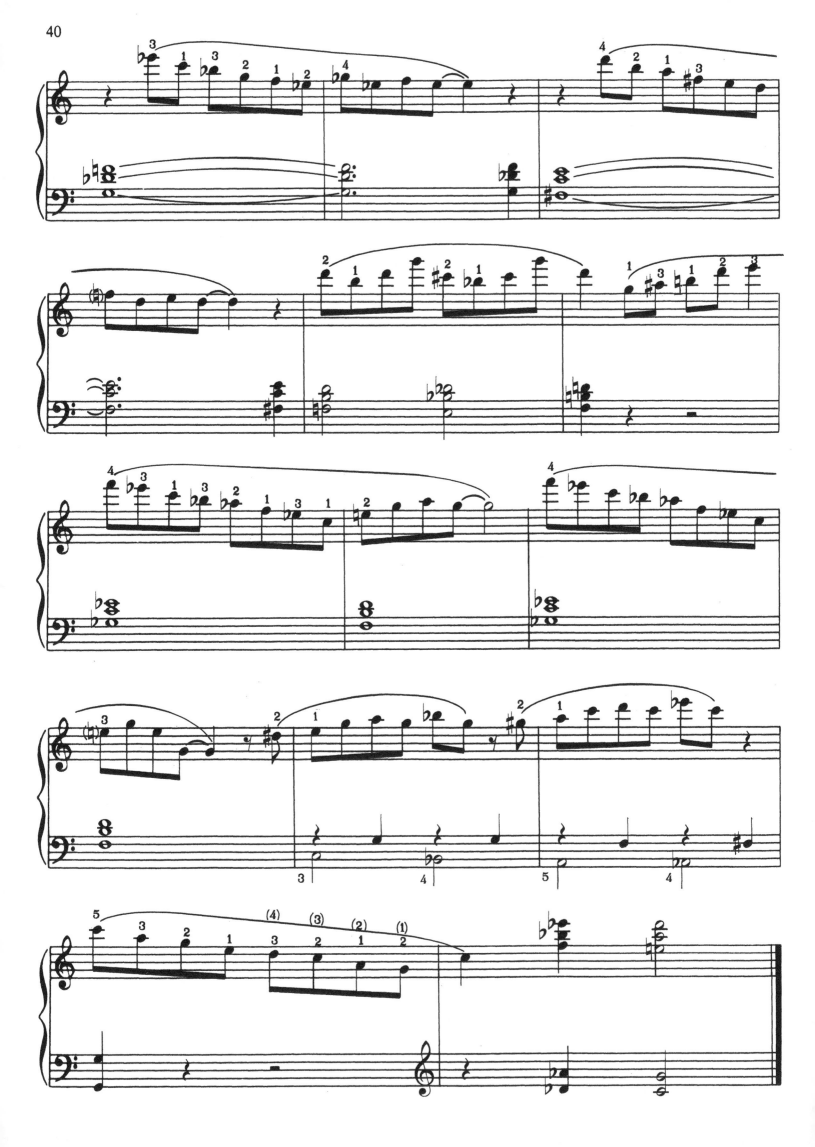